The Ogres' Magic Clubs 도깨비 방망이
The Tiger and the Dried Persimmons 호랑이와 곶감

Adapted by Duane Vorhees & Mark Mueller

Illustrated by Yon-kyong Kim

 Hollym

Carlsbad, CA and Seoul

The Ogres' Magic Clubs

A long time ago, there were two brothers who lived in a small village. The oldest was very greedy and lazy while the youngest was very kind and diligent.

One day, younger brother went to the mountains to gather some wood. After he gathered together a big load, he sat in the shade and wiped the sweat from his face.

At that moment, something hit the top of his head.

"Ouch! What is this? Ah, it's a hazelnut. I'll give it to my father." He decided and put it in his pocket.

 도깨비 방망이 •••

옛날, 어느 마을에 게으르고 욕심 많은 형과 부지런하고 마음씨 착한 아우가 살고 있었습니다.

어느 날, 산에 나무를 하러 간 아우는 나무를 한 짐 해 놓고, 그늘에 앉아 얼굴에 흐르는 땀을 닦고 있었습니다.

바로 그때 뭔가 머리를 딱 때리고 떨어졌습니다.

"아야! 이게 뭐지? 아, 개암이구나. 아버지께 갖다 드려야겠다."

아우는 개암을 주워 주머니에 넣었습니다.

Plop! Another hazelnut fell on his head.

Then he thought, "I'll give this one to my mother." And he put it in his pocket, too.

Plop! Plop! This time, two hazelnuts fell together.

"Wow!" exclaimed the younger brother. "This is my lucky day! These two nuts are for my older brother and me."

Soon, the sun started to set behind the mountain and it became very dark. To make matters worse, big, thick drops of rain started to fall.

The younger brother quickly picked up the load of wood and put it on his shoulders.

The raindrops became even bigger.

툭! 개암 한 개가 또 머리 위에 떨어졌습니다.

"이건 어머니 갖다 드려야지."

아우는 개암을 주워서 주머니에 넣었습니다.

투둑! 이번에는 개암 두 개가 한꺼번에 떨어졌습니다.

"와! 오늘은 재수가 좋은 날이구나. 이건 형님하고 내가 먹어야지."

어느새 해가 뉘엿뉘엿 넘어가고 주위가 어두워졌습니다. 그런데 엎친 데 덮쳐 갑자기 굵은 빗방울이 후드득 떨어지기 시작했습니다.

아우는 재빨리 나뭇짐을 들어 어깨에 멨습니다.

빗방울은 점점 더 굵어졌습니다.

"Where can I get out of this rain?" he wondered as he wandered around the mountains, with his feet slipping and sliding on the wet leaves.

Finally, he came to a small cottage hidden in the woods.

"Whew! At last I've found a place to rest for a while," he thought and he quickly went inside.

The place looked like it had not been lived in for a long, long time.

But it wasn't long before he heard someone tramping. "What kind of people would live here? They must be thieves!" he thought, looking for a place to hide. He quickly climbed up onto a beam high above the floor.

"어디 비를 피할 곳이 없을까?"

아우는 젖은 풀잎에 주르륵주르륵 미끄러지며 산길을 헤맸습니다.

그러다가 마침내 숲 속에 있는 조그만 오두막집을 발견했습니다.

"휴, 잘됐다. 저기서 잠시 쉬었다 가자."

아우는 얼른 집 안으로 들어갔습니다.

그 집은 오랫동안 사람이 살지 않은 것 같았습니다.

그러나 조금 뒤, 쿵쿵 걷는 소리가 들렸습니다.

"웬 사람들이지, 도둑이 틀림없어!"

아우는 허둥지둥 숨을 곳을 찾다가 마루에 있는 대들보 위로 재빨리 올라갔습니다.

A group of figures burst into the dark cottage, laughing, "A-ho-ho-ho, a-hee-hee-hee...."

When he looked down and saw them, the younger brother was so surprised that he almost fell off the beam.

They were not people at all! They were a bunch of ogres, with horns on their heads.

The younger brother shook with fear.

Then one of the ogres shouted, "Well, shall we begin our game?"

The ogres struck the floor with their clubs as they sang:

"Gold, gold, come ye forth!

Silver, silver, come ye out!"

"으하하하하 낄낄낄⋯⋯."

한 무리가 왁자지껄 어두운 집 안으로 들어왔습니다.

아래를 내려다본 아우는 깜짝 놀라 하마터면 대들보에서 떨어질 뻔했습니다.

그 무리는 사람이 아니라 머리에 뿔이 달린 도깨비들이었습니다.

아우는 너무 무서워서 부들부들 떨었습니다.

"자, 이제 슬슬 놀아 볼까?"

한 도깨비가 소리치자, 도깨비들이 모두 방망이로 마룻바닥을 두드리며 노래를 부르기 시작했습니다.

"금 나와라, 뚝딱! 은 나와라, 뚝딱!"

And every time the ogres hit their clubs on something, gold and silver coins shot out.

The younger brother watched in fascination as the ogres played their greedy game.

They were having so much fun that they started to skip about and dance, all the time singing their magic song and striking things with their clubs.

The younger brother had forgotten his fear, but he suddenly realized that he was quite hungry. Without a second thought, he took out one of the hazelnuts and tried to break it open with his teeth.

Crack! The hazelnut broke open.

신기하게도 도깨비들이 방망이를 두드릴 때마다 금화와 은화가 좌르르 쏟아져 나왔습니다.

아우는 도깨비들이 노는 모습을 넋을 잃고 쳐다보았습니다.

도깨비들은 흥에 겨워 덩실덩실 춤까지 추면서, 쉬지 않고 계속 방망이를 두드리며 노래를 불렀습니다.

무서움도 다 잊은 아우는 갑자기 배가 고파져 자기도 모르게 개암 한 개를 꺼내서 꽉 깨물 었습니다.

그러자 '따악' 하며 개암이 쪼개졌습니다.

The ogres stopped in their tracks. "What was that noise?" one of them exclaimed.

"Oh! We must have hit the cottage too many times! It must be falling down!" a second ogre cried.

"Hurry! Run! Get out before the house falls down on us!" yelled a third ogre. And the ogres all rushed out of the house as fast as they could run.

The younger brother was also frightened and very confused. He stayed right where he was on top of the beam.

Looking down, though, he could see the magical clubs which the ogres had left.

신나게 놀던 도깨비들이 우뚝 멈춰 섰습니다.

"이게 무슨 소리지?"

"우리가 너무 많이 두드려 대서 집이 무너지려고 하나 봐."

"서둘러! 집이 무너지기 전에 어서 도망가자!"

도깨비들이 모두 우르르 집 밖으로 뛰어나갔습니다.

아우는 어리둥절하고 겁이 나서 대들보 위에 가만히 엎드려 있었습니다.

마루 위에는 도깨비들이 도망가면서 두고 간 요술 방망이들만 어지럽게 널려 있었습니다.

When the morning sunbeams started to glow through the door, the younger brother, who had slept all night curled up on the beam, finally decided to come down.

Gold and silver coins covered the entire floor.

The younger brother laughed as he thought, "What foolish ogres! They left the cottage without taking any of their riches with them."

Then, just for fun, he picked up one of the clubs and hit it against the floor. As he did so, he repeated the words that he had heard the ogres sing:

"Gold, gold, come ye forth!"

And just as the club hit the floor, gold coins came pouring out.

So he took the ogre's magic club home with him.

아침 햇살이 문틈으로 쏟아져 들어오기 시작하자, 밤새 대들보 위에서 웅크리고 잠을 잔 아우는 슬슬 아래로 내려갔습니다.

마루 위에는 금화와 은화가 가득했습니다.

"도깨비들은 참 어리석구나, 이 많은 보물들을 그냥 버리고 가다니……."

아우는 장난삼아 방망이를 하나 들어서 마룻바닥에 두드리며 도깨비들이 부른 노래도 따라 해 보았습니다.

"금 나와라, 뚝딱!"

그러자 금화가 좌르르 쏟아져 나왔습니다.

아우는 도깨비 방망이를 가지고 집으로 돌아갔습니다.

The younger brother became very rich.

His older brother was unbearably jealous of his brother's wealth.

One day, the older brother lazily wandered up the mountain to gather wood, as his younger brother had done.

When he got to the forest, he stretched out on the path and took a nap.

The day slowly got dark.

When the older brother finally started to wake up, a hazelnut landed with a thud right in front of him.

"He, he! This will taste good. I'll eat it later." And he put the nut in his pocket.

아우는 엄청난 부자가 되었습니다.

형은 부자가 된 아우를 보자 샘이 나서 견딜 수 없었습니다.

그래서 아우처럼 나무를 하러 어슬렁어슬렁 산으로 올라갔습니다.

숲에 들어간 형은 벌렁 누워 쿨쿨 낮잠을 잤습니다.

날이 어둑어둑 저물어 갔습니다.

형이 부스스 일어나자 때마침 개암 한 개가 바로 앞에 툭 떨어졌습니다.

"히히, 맛있겠다. 이따가 먹어야지."

형은 개암을 주머니에 넣었습니다.

Another hazelnut fell down. "Wow! Look at this!" he exclaimed. "Now I have another one to eat!" He put it in his pocket.

Soon it became very dark, and the older brother stumbled his way through the forest. He reached the small, remote cottage.

When he got there, he climbed up to the beam and lay down to rest some more.

After a short while, a group of ogres rushed in.

Then they all swung their clubs in the air as they sang:

"Gold, gold. Come ye forth! Oh, silver. Come ye out!"

The ogres jumped and danced as they pounded their clubs.

개암이 또 한 개 툭 떨어졌습니다.

"와! 이것도 나중에 먹어야지."

형은 또 개암을 주워 주머니에 집어넣었습니다.

이윽고 날이 어두워지자, 형은 숲 속을 헤매다 마침내 작은 오두막집을 찾아냈습니다.

집에 들어선 형은 대들보 위로 올라가 드러누웠습니다.

잠시 후, 도깨비 무리가 우르르 뛰어 들어왔습니다.

도깨비들은 방망이를 허공에 휘두르며 노래를 불렀습니다.

"금 나와라, 뚝딱! 얼쑤. 은 나와라, 뚝딱! 얼쑤."

그리고 방망이 장단에 맞추어 덩실덩실 춤도 추었습니다.

The older brother watched the scene below with keen interest. Remembering his younger brother's story, he suddenly had an idea. "If I crack open a hazelnut, I will scare away the ogres! Then all their clubs will be mine!"

So he took a nut from his pocket and bit down on it with all his might. There was a loud cracking sound as the hazelnut split open.

The ogres suddenly stopped playing and stood still.

"What was that noise?" asked one. "I bet it was that man who played a trick on us," said another. "Come on everyone. Let's catch him!" shouted a third.

The ogres started rummaging every corner of the house.

아래에서 벌어지고 있는 광경을 아주 재미있게 구경하던 형은 아우가 들려준 이야기가 퍼뜩 떠올랐습니다.

'이제 내가 개암을 깨물면, 도깨비들이 놀라 달아날 테고, 그러면 저 도깨비 방망이들은 모두 내 것이 되는 거야!'

형이 주머니에서 개암을 꺼내 힘껏 깨물자 '따악' 하는 소리가 크게 났습니다.

그 순간 도깨비들은 놀이를 멈추고 제자리에 섰습니다.

"이게 무슨 소리지?"

"우리를 속였던 그놈이 분명해!"

"자, 모두들 어서 그놈을 잡아라!"

도깨비들은 온 집 안을 샅샅이 뒤지기 시작했습니다.

The older brother tried to stay perfectly still on the beam, but he shivered and quivered in fear.

One of the ogres saw him move and shouted, "Ah-ha! There he is!"

The older brother cried and cried as he begged, "Please, please, let me go!"

"You stupid man," they shouted, "you stole one of our clubs, and you still think we'll just let you go? Let's give him a good beating."

And they hit the older brother with their clubs as hard as they could.

After the ogres beat the greedy older brother over and over, they let him leave.

The older brother returned home and he never went back to that shack in the woods again.

형은 대들보 위에서 움직이지 않고 가만히 있으려고 했지만 겁에 질려 몸이 덜덜 떨렸습니다.

"아하, 놈이 저기 있다!"

형을 찾아낸 도깨비가 소리쳤습니다.

"아이고, 제발 살려 주십시오."

형은 살려 달라고 울며불며 애원했습니다.

"네 이놈! 우리 방망이를 훔쳐 가고도 성할 줄 알았느냐? 어디 혼 좀 나 봐라."

도깨비들은 방망이로 형을 펑펑 두들겨 팼습니다.

욕심쟁이 형은 도깨비들에게 흠씬 두들겨 맞고서야 겨우 풀려났습니다.

집에 돌아온 형은 두 번 다시 그 오두막집을 찾아가지 않았습니다.

The Tiger and the Dried Persimmons

Once upon a time, in a valley deep in the mountains, there lived a huge tiger.

He always walked around and boasted about his great strength, saying, "I dare anyone to match my strength."

When the other animals on the mountain heard him, they all shrieked and ran away.

 호랑이와 곶감 ···

옛날 옛적에, 깊은 산골짜기에 키다란 호랑이 한 마리가 살고 있었습니다.

호랑이는 자기가 힘이 세다는 것을 뽐내고 다녔습니다.

"나보다 힘센 놈 있으면 어디 나와 봐라."

산 속의 작은 짐승들은 호랑이 소리가 들리면 비명을 지르며 허둥지둥 달아났습니다.

There was a very cold winter one year.

The snow piled up over many days, so the tiger could not dig out of his cave.

"I'm so hungry I can't stand it any longer," he grumbled, and he slowly and painfully got out of his cave.

The thick snow made the entire mountain white.

"Oh, no!" the tiger mumbled. "Even though I'm very hungry, there's nothing to eat!" As he wandered around the mountains, every few footsteps he sank deep down into the snow.

어느 해 추운 겨울이었습니다.

며칠 동안 눈이 내려서 호랑이는 동굴 밖으로 나갈 수 없었습니다.

"이거 배가 고파서 더 이상은 못 견디겠는데……."

호랑이는 힘을 내어 간신히 동굴을 빠져나왔습니다.

온 산이 눈으로 하얗게 뒤덮여 있었습니다.

"아이고, 배가 고픈데 먹을 게 아무것도 없잖아."

호랑이는 눈 속에 풀풀 빠지면서 산 속을 돌아다녔습니다.

By the time darkness fell, the tiger had reached the village which lay at the foot of the mountain.

He snooped and poked around until he found a barn outside a farmhouse. A fat cow was asleep inside.

"That should make a good meal!" he said, licking his chops.

Just at that moment, the tiger heard a small child crying inside the house.

"Eh! What's that noise?" thought the tiger. He sneaked up to the room in which the child was crying.

날이 저물 무렵, 호랑이는 산 아래 있는 마을에 이르렀습니다.

이집 저집을 기웃거리던 호랑이는 어느 농가의 외양간을 찾아냈습니다.

외양간 안에는 살찐 소 한 마리가 쿨쿨 잠을 자고 있었습니다.

"아주 먹음직스럽군!"

호랑이는 입맛을 다셨습니다.

바로 그때 집 안에서 어린아이 울음소리가 들렸습니다.

'에! 이게 무슨 소리지?'

호랑이는 울음소리가 나는 방으로 살금살금 다가갔습니다.

In the room a mother was trying to make her child stop crying. The mother said, "Oh! look! There's a monster! You had better stop crying, or he'll get you!"

But the child kept crying. So the mother said, "There's a tiger outside! If you keep crying, he'll come and eat you!"

When the tiger heard this, he was surprised. "How can she know I am here?" he wondered. "I must be more careful."

The child cried even louder. "What's this?" thought the tiger. He didn't like the idea of a child not being afraid of a tiger.

방에서는 엄마가 우는 아이를 달래고 있었습니다.

"저기 좀 봐! 도깨비가 왔다. 어서 그쳐야지. 안 그러면 도깨비가 잡아간다."

아이가 울음을 그치지 않자 엄마는 이렇게 말했습니다.

"아가, 밖에 호랑이가 왔다! 계속 울면 호랑이가 잡아먹는다."

그 말을 들은 호랑이는 깜짝 놀랐습니다.

'어라? 내가 온 걸 어떻게 알았지? 좀 더 조심히 다녀야겠군.'

아이는 더 크게 울었습니다.

'뭐지?'

호랑이는 아이가 자신을 무서워하지 않자 기분이 상했습니다.

The child cried and cried.

Finally, the mother pulled out something and showed it to the child. "Look! Here is a dried persimmon!" she said. The child immediately stopped crying.

The tiger, who had been listening to all of this from outside the room, became very frightened.

"A persimmon?" he thought and thought, "A persimmon must be a very scary beast since it stopped that child from crying. It must be more powerful and frightening than I am, since I didn't scare the child at all. If I dawdle around here very long, the persimmon might eat me!"

The tiger walked very carefully back to the barn.

아이는 계속 울어 댔습니다.

마침내 엄마는 아이에게 뭔가를 꺼내 보이며 말했습니다.

"자, 곶감이다."

신기하게도 아이는 울음을 뚝 그쳤습니다.

바깥에서 듣고 있던 호랑이는 덜컥 겁이 났습니다.

'곶감? 곶감이 대체 어떻게 생긴 놈이기에 저 아이가 울음을 그쳤을까? 나보다 힘도 세고 무서운 놈인 게 틀림없어. 여기서 꾸물거리다가는 곶감에게 잡아먹히겠는걸!'

호랑이는 슬슬 뒷걸음질을 쳐서 외양간으로 돌아갔습니다.

It was very dark inside the barn.

At that moment, a big black thing crept through the barn door. "Oh, no! That thing must be the persimmon!" thought the tiger. The tiger was so scared it couldn't move.

The black shape walked with big strides up to where the tiger was sitting. It reached down and very gently rubbed across the tiger's back. Then it said, "This one's really nice and fat!"

The tiger was so scared that it just stood there shaking.

외양간은 아주 어두웠습니다.

그때 외양간 안으로 웬 시커먼 것이 불쑥 들어왔습니다.

'이키, 저놈이 바로 곶감이구나!'

호랑이는 무서워서 꼼짝도 못하고 서 있었습니다.

시커먼 것은 호랑이에게 성큼성큼 다가와 호랑이 등을 살살 쓰다듬었습니다.

"그놈 참 살도 포동포동하게 쪘네."

호랑이는 겁에 질려서 부들부들 떨었습니다.

The big black thing that the tiger thought was a persimmon was really a thief who had come to steal the cow.

It was so dark that the thief couldn't see very well inside the barn.

He thought the furry tiger was the cow. So the thief gently led the tiger outside.

Once outside the barn, the thief reached down and patted the tiger, but this time he noticed that the fur he touched wasn't cow fur. He looked down and thought, "Oh, no! This isn't a cow at all. It's a tiger!" The thief was so surprised.

The tiger, on the other hand, thought that the persimmon had gotten him for sure. He closed his eyes and thought, "Oh no! The ferocious persimmon is surely going to eat me!"

호랑이가 곶감이라고 생각한 시커먼 것은 사실 소를 훔치러 온 도둑이었습니다.

소도둑은 너무 어두워서 털이 부드러운 호랑이를 소라고 생각하고 조용히 외양간 밖으로 끌고 나왔습니다.

밖으로 나와 호랑이를 토닥이던 소도둑은 깜짝 놀랐습니다.

'이키! 이건 소가 아니라 호랑이잖아!'

한편, 호랑이는 호랑이대로 꼼짝없이 곶감에게 잡혔다고 생각했습니다.

'아, 나는 이제 곶감에게 잡아먹히는구나!'

호랑이는 두 눈을 꼭 감았습니다.

The thief was too afraid to move, so he just stood still next to the tiger.

The tiger thought, "This is my chance!" And he jumped free and tried to run away.

But when the thief felt the tiger start to move, he thought that the tiger was going to try to grab and eat him. So he immediately jumped onto the tiger's back and held on for dear life.

소도둑은 너무 무서워서 옴짝달싹 못하고 호랑이 옆에 서 있었습니다.

'옳지, 이때다!'

호랑이는 소도둑이 머뭇거리는 틈을 타서 재빨리 도망치려고 했습니다.

그런데 소도둑은 호랑이가 움직이자 자기를 잡아먹으려는 줄 알고, 얼른 호랑이 등에 올라타 죽을 힘을 다해 꽉 붙잡았습니다.

The scared tiger leaped up and down and ran around in circles trying to throw the thief off his back.

But this only made the thief hold on even tighter.

The tiger then ran wildly, thinking, "No matter how strong a persimmon is, it will surely fall off when I run as fast as I can."

So the tiger used all of his strength to run as fast as an arrow.

The tiger, with the thief on his back, quickly ran out of the village and turned onto a mountain path.

호랑이는 등에서 소도둑을 떨어뜨리려고 펄쩍펄쩍 뛰고, 뱅뱅 돌기도 했습니다.

하지만 그럴수록 소도둑은 호랑이 등을 더욱 단단히 붙잡았습니다.

호랑이는 마구 달리기 시작했습니다.

'제아무리 힘센 곶감이라도 이렇게 빨리 달리면 떨어지고 말겠지?'

호랑이는 온 힘을 다해 쏜살같이 달렸습니다.

호랑이와 호랑이 등에 탄 소도둑은 순식간에 마을을 벗어나 산길로 접어들었습니다.

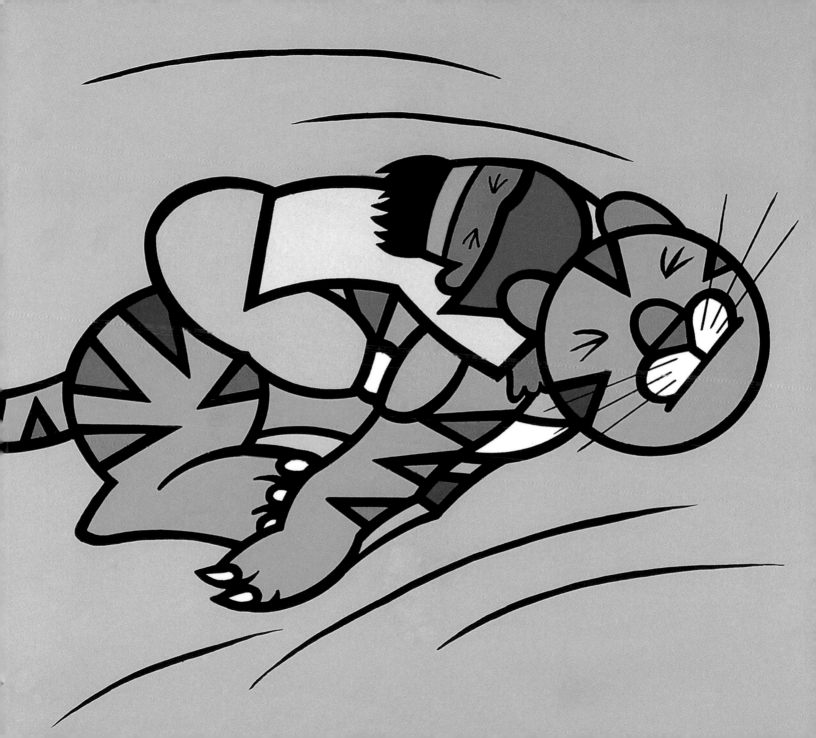

Dawn came and the day grew bright.

The thief looked above his head and saw a branch of a tree hanging down.

He reached up and grabbed the branch. He held the branch tightly.

But the tiger kept running and didn't look back. After he ran a while longer, though, he noticed that his back felt lighter, so he stopped running and heaved a great sigh of relief.

"Whew!" he sighed. "That was close! Today I was nearly eaten by a persimmon."

이윽고 날이 밝아 오기 시작했습니다.

소도둑은 고개를 들어 길게 드리워져 있는 나뭇가지를 보고 재빨리 손을 뻗어 대롱대롱 매달렸습니다.

호랑이는 뒤도 돌아보지 않고 한참을 달리나가 등이 가벼워진 것을 알아채고 안도의 한숨을 내쉬었습니다.

"휴, 하마터면 오늘 곶감이란 놈에게 잡아먹힐 뻔했네."